Thinking Critically:
The COVID-19 Pandemic

Kathryn Hulick

ReferencePoint Press®

San Diego, CA

© 2023 ReferencePoint Press, Inc.
Printed in the United States

For more information, contact:
ReferencePoint Press, Inc.
PO Box 27779
San Diego, CA 92198
www.ReferencePointPress.com

LIBRARY OF CONGRESS CATALOGING-IN-PUBLICATION DATA

Names: Hulick, Kathryn, author.
Title: Thinking critically : the COVID-19 pandemic / by Kathryn Hulick.
Description: San Diego, CA : ReferencePoint Press, Inc., 2023. | Series:
    Thinking critically | Includes bibliographical references and index.
Identifiers: LCCN 2022003555 (print) | LCCN 2022003556 (ebook) | ISBN
    9781678203160 (library binding) | ISBN 9781678203177 (ebook)
Subjects: LCSH: COVID-19 Pandemic, 2020---United States--Juvenile
    literature. | COVID-19 (Disease)--Government policy--United
    States--Juvenile literature. | COVID-19 (Disease)--Economic
    aspects--United States--Juvenile literature. | COVID-19
    (Disease)--Social aspects--United States--Juvenile literature. | Medical
    policy--United States--Decision making--Juvenile literature.
Classification: LCC RA644.C67 H852 2023 (print) | LCC RA644.C67 (ebook) |
    DDC 614.5/92414--dc23/eng/20220309
LC record available at https://lccn.loc.gov/2022003555
LC ebook record available at https://lccn.loc.gov/2022003556

Contents

Foreword   4
Overview: The COVID-19 Pandemic   6

Chapter One: Do Pandemic Mandates Violate Individual Rights?
The Debate at a Glance   12
Pandemic Mandates Violate Individual Rights   13
Pandemic Mandates Protect Public Health   19

Chapter Two: Have Lockdowns Been Worth the Economic and Social Harm?
The Debate at a Glance   25
Lockdowns Saved Lives and Communities Bounced Back   26
Lockdowns Did More Harm than Good   32

Chapter Three: Has Vaccine Distribution Failed?
The Debate at a Glance   38
Vaccine Distribution Has Failed   39
Vaccines Reached Billions and Saved Lives   45

Source Notes   51
COVID-19 Facts   55
Related Organizations and Websites   57
For Further Research   59
Index   61
Picture Credits   64
About the Author   64

Foreword

"Literacy is the most basic currency of the knowledge economy we're living in today." Barack Obama (at the time a senator from Illinois) spoke these words during a 2005 speech before the American Library Association. One question raised by this statement is: What does it mean to be a literate person in the twenty-first century?

E.D. Hirsch Jr., author of *Cultural Literacy: What Every American Needs to Know*, answers the question this way: "To be culturally literate is to possess the basic information needed to thrive in the modern world. The breadth of the information is great, extending over the major domains of human activity from sports to science."

But literacy in the twenty-first century goes beyond the accumulation of knowledge gained through study and experience and expanded over time. Now more than ever literacy requires the ability to sift through and evaluate vast amounts of information and, as the authors of the Common Core State Standards state, to "demonstrate the cogent reasoning and use of evidence that is essential to both private deliberation and responsible citizenship in a democratic republic."

The Thinking Critically series challenges students to become discerning readers, to think independently, and to engage and develop their skills as critical thinkers. Through a narrative-driven, pro/con format, the series introduces students to the complex issues that dominate public discourse—topics such as gun control and violence, social networking, and medical marijuana. All chapters revolve around a single, pointed question such as Can Stronger Gun Control Measures Prevent Mass Shootings?, or Does Social Networking Benefit Society?, or Should Medical Marijuana Be Legalized? This inquiry-based approach introduces student

4

researchers to core issues and concerns on a given topic. Each chapter includes one part that argues the affirmative and one part that argues the negative—all written by a single author. With the single-author format the predominant arguments for and against an issue can be synthesized into clear, accessible discussions supported by details and evidence including relevant facts, direct quotes, current examples, and statistical illustrations. All volumes include focus questions to guide students as they read each pro/con discussion, a list of key facts, and an annotated list of related organizations and websites for conducting further research.

The authors of the Common Core State Standards have set out the particular qualities that a literate person in the twenty-first century must have. These include the ability to think independently, establish a base of knowledge across a wide range of subjects, engage in open-minded but discerning reading and listening, know how to use and evaluate evidence, and appreciate and understand diverse perspectives. The new Thinking Critically series supports these goals by providing a solid introduction to the study of pro/con issues.

The COVID-19 Pandemic

"No one deserves to feel like they're slowly being suffocated to death," says Ganeene Starling. Yet that is exactly how she felt as she lay in a hospital bed in July 2021, deathly ill with COVID-19. A hissing oxygen machine kept her alive. Starling, a mother of eight who lives in Florida, had decided not to get vaccinated against COVID-19. She had feared the possible side effects of the vaccine. Then she fell sick and only barely pulled through. This terrifying experience changed her mind about vaccination. "I was so against this vaccine," she says. "And I am begging people to get it now. You might not be as lucky as I was. You might die."[1]

As of February 2022, the COVID-19 pandemic has taken the lives of nearly 6 million people around the world. Many got sick before vaccines were even available. The victims include Dez-Ann Romain, a thirty-six-year-old high school principal in Brooklyn, New York. Roberto Stella was a sixty-seven-year-old doctor in a town outside of Milan, Italy. Ken Shimura was a seventy-year-old comedian in Tokyo, Japan. Gita Ramjee was a sixty-three-year-old medical researcher in South Africa. Isai Morocho was a sixteen-year-old high school junior from Wisconsin. The names go on and on, all unique human beings who never got to realize all of their dreams and who left grief-stricken family and friends behind.

The pandemic did not impact everyone evenly. Elderly people and men were at greater risk from the disease than younger people, children, and women. People with health conditions such as cancer, heart disease, obesity, and Down syndrome, among others, also faced a greater risk of severe illness or death. The risk of exposure was higher for those who lived or worked in communal settings, such as hospitals, nursing homes, or prisons. In addition, marginalized or impoverished communities suffered much greater losses than privileged or wealthy ones.

The Arrival of a Pandemic

The disease COVID-19 is caused by a virus named SARS-CoV-2. It is a coronavirus in the same family of viruses that includes the common cold. No one knows exactly where SARS-CoV-2 came from, but most experts agree that bats were the likely source. All viruses naturally mutate, or change, over time. Sometimes a mutation allows a virus to infect new hosts or spread more easily. In late 2019, the SARS-CoV-2 virus gained the ability to infect humans and to pass from one human to another.

This fateful event happened in Wuhan, China, most likely at a market where people buy animals and fresh meat. Throughout the month of December 2019, doctors in Wuhan noticed more and more patients with similar symptoms arriving in hospitals. Chinese officials reported the outbreak to the World Health Organization (WHO) on December 31, 2019.

By mid-January 2020, cases began showing up in other countries, including Nepal, Vietnam, and South Korea, as well as in the United States, France, and Italy. A few weeks later, it was spreading widely all over the world. WHO named the disease COVID-19 in February and declared it a pandemic on March 11. In a statement, WHO wrote, "Pandemic is not a word to use lightly or carelessly. . . . We have called every day for countries to take urgent and aggressive action. We have rung the alarm bell loud and clear."[2]

> "Pandemic is not a word to use lightly or carelessly. . . . We have called every day for countries to take urgent and aggressive action. We have rung the alarm bell loud and clear."[2]
>
> —World Health Organization

Panic Around the World

In early 2020, experts did not yet understand how the new virus spread or how people should best protect themselves. Many governments started quarantining patients and their close contacts. Many instituted travel bans or ordered lockdowns that prevented people from gathering or going to school or work.

Everywhere, people panicked. In the United States, hand sanitizer, toilet paper, and groceries flew off shelves. Misinformation, fake cures, and rumors polluted the internet. Some people wrongly believed the entire pandemic was a hoax. Sadly, it was not. Some blamed China, but, in fact, Chinese scientists had taken important first steps in identifying the new virus and alerting the world. In New York City, hospitals ran out of beds and ventilators. Kids missed school and grown-ups lost their jobs. Entire industries transformed as people stopped going to restaurants or traveling but took up baking and meeting on Zoom. People practiced social distancing and got used to wearing face masks if they had to go out in public. Meanwhile, pharmaceutical companies raced to develop vaccines. The first shots were given in December 2020, exactly one year after the pandemic had begun.

The Danger Was Not Over

Many people thought that vaccines would put an end to the pandemic. Unfortunately, that was not the case. The vaccines certainly helped save lives, but even as millions of people showed up for their shots, others continued to sicken and die. Many of them could not get vaccinated or, like Starling, feared vaccination. By February 2022, around nine hundred thousand Americans had died of COVID-19. The death rate at this point was higher than in any other wealthy nation, mostly due to a relatively low vaccination rate. Lockdowns, travel restrictions, mask mandates, and other preventative measures came and went throughout the pandemic.

The virus also mutated into new forms. Two of those forms, Delta and Omicron, became widespread. The Delta variant, which first emerged in India in late 2020, was more contagious and could even infect vaccinated people. This is called a break-through infection. Omicron was first detected in Botswana and South Africa in November 2021. This variant was even more con-tagious than Delta and also more likely to cause breakthrough infections. However, Omicron tended to cause milder symptoms, with less risk of hospitalization or death. Vaccinated people were at a much lower risk of severe illness or death from either variant.

How COVID-19 Spreads

Experts now understand very well how the SARS-CoV-2 virus spreads and how people can protect themselves and their loved ones. The virus spreads most easily through the air, riding inside tiny droplets that fly out when a person coughs, sneezes, speaks, sings, or breathes. If other people are standing nearby, the drop-lets may land on their faces or they may breathe them in. The more virus-carrying droplets that enter the eyes, nose, mouth, or airway, the more likely it is that the person will be infected.

Some of these droplets are so tiny that they remain floating in the air. In an indoor space without good ventilation, they may last for up to three hours. If an indoor space is crowded, there is a higher chance that some people there are infected and adding to the amount of the virus accumulating in the air. Outside, air currents scatter any infected droplets quickly, so it is much less likely for the disease to spread outside. Droplets containing the virus can also accumulate on people's hands or, more rarely, on surfaces or objects. If people touch their faces with contaminated hands, this could also cause an infection.

How to Stay Safe

These facts about transmission make it much easier to under-stand the recommended prevention measures. First of all, the Centers for Disease Control and Prevention (CDC) recommend that everyone get a COVID-19 vaccine as soon as they are able.

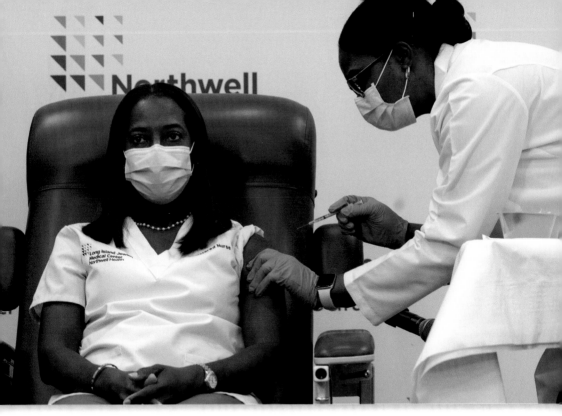

Sandra Lindsay (left), a nurse at Long Island Jewish Medical Center in New York City, was the first American to receive a COVID-19 vaccine. By publicizing her action, and by appearing in Zoom town halls and other events, she hoped to ease people's fears about the vaccine.

The vaccine teaches the body's immune system to recognize and destroy the virus before it can cause an infection. If an infection does occur, it will likely be mild. Rigorous testing has proved that these vaccines are effective and safe. In the United States, as of February 2022, the Food and Drug Administration (FDA) had approved them for everyone ages five and older.

As of early 2022, the CDC recommended that everyone (even vaccinated people) wear a mask in indoor public places in communities where COVID-19 is actively spreading. Mask wearing is important because a mask is like a wall that most droplets cannot get through. Masks are more important indoors because the risk of transmission is so much higher there. The CDC also recommends staying 6 feet (2 m) apart from others and avoiding crowds. The farther apart people are, the less likely it is that they will exchange any droplets. Regular handwashing (twenty seconds with soap and water) or hand sanitizing is also recommended. So is covering any coughs or sneezes. Gathering outdoors or opening windows when indoors increases air flow, which carries droplets away so they do not hang around.

Finally, knowing the symptoms of COVID-19 and getting tested can help keep people safe. The symptoms include fever, shortness of breath, cough, tiredness, body aches, headache, loss of taste or smell, sore throat, congestion, nausea, and diarrhea. The CDC urges that anyone who has any of these symptoms get tested. They should also isolate themselves while waiting for the test result in case it is positive. Some people who are infected and contagious do not feel sick. Only a test can tell if a person has COVID-19 or not. The CDC recommends that people test themselves before going to indoor gatherings.

Following all these safety recommendations has not been easy. Governments, public health experts, and citizens have disagreed on the most effective ways to respond to the pandemic. Every approach has to balance public safety with personal freedom and economic cost. As a result, leaders around the world faced many difficult decisions. They put many controversial mandates and policies in place. The response to COVID-19 certainly has not been perfect. But the world has learned a lot about how to face a common enemy and survive through an extremely trying and difficult time.

Chapter One

Do Pandemic Mandates Violate Individual Rights?

Pandemic Mandates Violate Individual Rights

- Health care decisions are personal, private choices that should not be dictated by authorities.
- Mask and vaccine mandates are classic examples of government overreach.
- Mandates are not the best way to change people's behavior.
- Mandates can lead to discrimination and inequality.

The Debate at a Glance

Pandemic Mandates Protect Public Health

- A public health crisis outweighs individual rights.
- Some vulnerable people cannot make the choice to protect themselves.
- Mask and vaccine mandates save lives.

Pandemic Mandates Violate Individual Rights

"We're going to make sure people are able to make their own choices. We're not going to discriminate against people based on those choices, and you're going to have a right to operate in society."

—Ron DeSantis, governor of Florida

Quoted in Alana Wise, "The Political Fight Over Vaccine Mandates Deepens Despite Their Effectiveness," *Coronavirus Crisis,* National Public Radio, October 17, 2021. www.npr.org.

Consider these questions as you read:

1. Do you agree that vaccine mandates violate the right to bodily autonomy? Why or why not?
2. How persuasive is the argument that allowing the government to issue mandates during a pandemic will lead to even more restrictions on freedom or privacy after the pandemic ends?
3. How could vaccine passports divide society? Do you think vaccine passports should be against the law? Why or why not?

Editor's note: The discussion that follows presents common arguments made in support of this perspective, reinforced by facts, quotes, and examples taken from various sources.

To try to limit the impact of the COVID-19 pandemic, many governments, businesses, and organizations have ordered people to wear masks, prohibited large indoor gatherings, restricted people's travel, or required proof of vaccination. Although it is indeed important for people to protect themselves and others from this deadly contagious disease, no one should mandate these protections. "If you want to wear a mask, great. I will never look down on you, have anything bad to say to you, do what you want. But the mandates are what I disagree with and I don't think are right, especially now,"[3] Gina, a real estate agent in Pennsylvania, told Vox in 2020. Gina wore a mask at work, but she disagreed with the idea of mask mandates. Many people feel the same way.

Pandemic-related mandates are an attack on people's personal freedom and a classic case of government overreach. The COVID-19 pandemic can be managed effectively without bureaucratic requirements and rules. People should not be penalized or prevented from participating in society over health decisions that should be personal and private.

An Attack on Personal Freedom and Bodily Autonomy

Individualism, or the idea that every adult deserves to be treated as a self-sufficient person, is a core value in American culture. An individual should not be controlled by family, community, or any other group. Individualism is a cornerstone of democracy. Citizens in a free and democratic society should not to be told what to do—they should be given all the information they need to make their own decisions. The freedom to make decisions is especially important when it comes to personal health and bodily autonomy. Adults are responsible enough to educate themselves on how to best protect themselves and their families from COVID-19. Mandating protections violates their individual rights.

The US Constitution protects many individual rights under the Fourteenth Amendment, which says that states may not "deprive any person of life, liberty, or property, without due process of law."[4] The US Supreme Court has repeatedly interpreted this passage as protecting a person's right to privacy and bodily autonomy. In other words, people have the right to decide what happens to their own bodies. This has been a key issue in the fight for abortion rights and gay rights. A person also has the right to refuse unwanted medical treatment. In a 1990 decision, the Supreme Court said, "The forcible injection of medication into a noncon-

> "The forcible injection of medication into a nonconsenting person's body represents a substantial interference with that person's liberty."[5]
>
> —US Supreme Court

senting person's body represents a substantial interference with that person's liberty."[5]

COVID-19 vaccination involves injection with a needle. So, requiring someone to get injected amounts to a breach of that person's rights. Despite this issue, many employers began requiring proof of vaccination for all workers in the summer and fall of 2021. Protesters took to the streets to defend their rights. Many used the phrase "my body, my choice."[6] Olivia Ravadge was one of dozens who turned out to protest her company's vaccine mandate in October 2021. She said, "We should not be forced to put something in our body that we don't want to and we're going to stand behind that."[7] Another protester, Garth Bonbargen, said, "We're not anti-vax. . . . We're just pro-choice."[8]

Government Overreach

Many protesters argue that mandates are a slippery slope. If the government is allowed to mandate masks or vaccines now, then after the pandemic is over it may require people to surrender personal rights for other reasons. Michael Drodes was at the same protest with Ravadge and Bonbargen. He said, "I feel mandates in general upon free citizens of this country is unconstitutional and if it starts here, when does it end?"[9]

To help prevent government overreach, the US Constitution limits the powers of the federal government. States have something called police powers, which allow them to pass laws to protect the health and safety of the public, but the federal government does not. Despite this history, President Joe Biden tried to put several different vaccine mandates in place during 2021. One would require most businesses to make their employees show proof of vaccination or get tested regularly. The Supreme Court blocked this mandate in January 2022, decreeing that the federal government could not use its powers in this way.

States have taken very different stances on mandates. As of December 2021, twenty-five states and thirty-nine cities had required vaccination for some workers, often health care workers

Some Workers Would Rather Quit than Get Vaccinated

In October 2021 the Kaiser Family Foundation surveyed unvaccinated, employed Americans about what they would do if their employer mandated vaccination. Thirty-seven percent said they would leave their job rather than get the shot or get tested weekly. If weekly testing was not going to be an option, 72 percent said they would quit.

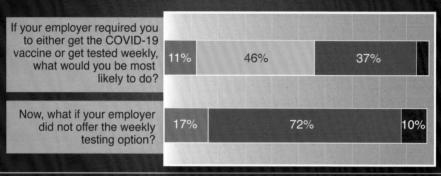

If your employer required you to either get the COVID-19 vaccine or get tested weekly, what would you be most likely to do?	11%	46%	37%	
Now, what if your employer did not offer the weekly testing option?	17%	72%		10%

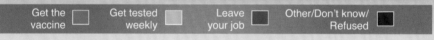

Get the vaccine ☐ Get tested weekly ☐ Leave your job ■ Other/Don't know/ Refused ■

Source: Liz Hamel et al., "KFF COVID-19 Vaccine Monitor: October 2021," Kaiser Family Foundation, October 28, 2021. www.kff.org.

or public employees. However, two states had banned private employers from requiring their workers to get vaccinated. In addition, at least a dozen states had passed laws to stop local health officials from issuing other types of mandates. In Arkansas and Ohio, health officials are not allowed to mandate mask wearing. In Tennessee, health officials cannot close schools.

Clearly, many Americans do not want the government meddling in their health decisions. Elise Stefanik, a representative from New York, said in a statement, "The American people should have the freedom to make the best decisions for their families, not be forced to comply with illegal mandates from a power hungry government."[10] Jim Banks, a repre-

> "The American people should have the freedom to make the best decisions for their families, not be forced to comply with illegal mandates from a power hungry government."[10]
>
> —Elise Stefanik, US representative from New York

sentative from Indiana, was even more straight to the point. He tweeted, "Vaccine mandates are unAmerican!"[11]

Troubling Consequences

Mandates, and especially vaccination mandates, have troubling consequences. Some people have already quit their jobs or have been terminated because they refused to comply with mandates. Karl Bohnak delivered weather forecasts on television in Michigan for thirty-three years, until he was fired in 2021 for refusing to get vaccinated. He says, "I felt it was my right as a human being and a citizen of the U.S. to decide what I put in my body."[12] Josephine Valdez, a thirty-year-old paraprofessional in the New York public school system, also lost her job for refusing the vaccine. When her students asked her why she had to leave, she told the New York Times, "I had to explain to them, the government doesn't own my body."[13] Others have gotten the shot only because they felt they had no other choice. A nurse in Las Vegas told the digital publication Government Executive that she got vaccinated, but she "feels controlled"[14] by her employer.

> "I felt it was my right as a human being and a citizen of the U.S. to decide what I put in my body."[12]
>
> —Karl Bohnak, former television weather forecaster in Michigan

Five states—California, Hawaii, New York, Oregon, and Washington—have created some form of what is called a vaccine passport. This is a physical card or an app that proves that the holder has been vaccinated and allows the person access to goods and services. Under this type of system, an unvaccinated person may be prevented from going to restaurants, traveling, shopping, or participating in numerous other daily activities. This is an alarming breach of civil rights, especially if some people are unable to access vaccines. Perhaps they cannot take time off of work or do not have transportation to a clinic. "The people who are immune will get all of the benefits and privileges that come with that while everybody else who's not immune will be in a second class status,"[15] says Esha Bhandari, a civil liberties expert at the American Civil Liberties Union (ACLU).

American society has worked very hard to do away with racist, sexist, and classist policies that divide people. Mandated mask wearing or vaccination creates a new form of social division. People deserve to make their own health care choices.

Pandemic Mandates Protect Public Health

"With freedom comes responsibility. The decision to be unvaccinated impacts someone else. Unvaccinated people spread the virus. . . . So please, exercise responsible judgment. Get vaccinated—for yourself, for the people you love, for your country."

—Joe Biden, president of the United States

Joe Biden, "Remarks by President Biden Laying Out the Next Steps in Our Effort to Get More Americans Vaccinated and Combat the Spread of the Delta Variant," White House Briefing Room, July 29, 2021. www.whitehouse.gov.

Consider these questions as you read:

1. Do you agree that public health outweighs individual rights during a pandemic? Why or why not?
2. Road safety laws and pandemic mandates limit personal freedom while reducing risk to others. What are some other rules that limit freedom but protect public health or safety? Why are these types of rules important?
3. How persuasive is the argument that vaccine mandates were successful? Explain your answer.

Editor's note: The discussion that follows presents common arguments made in support of this perspective, reinforced by facts, quotes, and examples taken from various sources.

The COVID-19 pandemic threw the globe into a state of emergency. As millions have sickened and died, leaders around the world have had to make difficult choices. Following the advice of experienced physicians, medical researchers, and public health officials, many governments and private organizations have mandated mask wearing, lockdowns, vaccination, and other measures. They have done this to slow the spread of the disease and save lives. Health experts overwhelmingly agree that vaccination is the best response to the COVID-19 pandemic. In the United States, plenty of doses are available, free of charge. Mandates are necessary to make sure these doses get to as many people as possible.

In a crisis such as this pandemic, public health outweighs individual rights. When President Joe Biden announced new vaccine mandates in September 2021, he explained, "This is not about freedom or personal choice. It's about protecting yourself and those around you—the people you work with, the people you care about, the people you love. My job as President is to protect all Americans."[16]

Freedom Does Not Include Endangering Others

People should have the freedom to make their own choices unless those choices may cause harm to others. Americans already observe many safety rules that help protect society. For example, speed limits and stop signs make public roads safer for everybody. US citizens do not have the freedom to drive recklessly and risk harming others. Refusing to wear a mask or get vaccinated during the COVID-19 pandemic similarly endangers others. Unmasked or unvaccinated people may have the right to risk getting infected themselves, but they do not have the right to risk infecting others.

The SARS-CoV-2 virus spreads extremely quickly and easily, even among people who show no signs of sickness. A person who feels perfectly healthy could infect several other people with COVID-19 before realizing that he or she is contagious. If that person wears a mask or—even better—gets vaccinated, he or she will be much less likely to spread the disease to others.

Unvaccinated people are also far more likely to get infected and end up in the hospital. These patients not only risk their own deaths but also pose a risk to others. When hospital overcrowding

Most Americans Are Willing to Sacrifice Personal Liberty to Support the Common Good

A majority of Americans are willing to accept vaccine or mask mandates in order to protect society. Two-thirds say that in general, requiring people to do things they don't want to do is acceptable if it supports the common good.

Which statement comes closer to your view, even if neither is exactly right?

Protecting personal liberty is more important, even if it does result in other people getting hurt

Protecting the common good is more important, even if that means requiring some people to do things they don't want to do

Thinking specifically about the COVID-19 vaccine, which statement comes closer to your view, even if neither is exactly right?

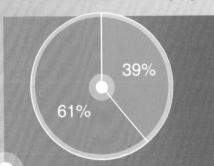

Protecting personal liberty is more important, and that means individuals should be able to choose whether or not to get the vaccine

Protecting the common good is more important, and that means individuals can be required to get the vaccine, absent a medical or religious exemption

Thinking specifically about requiring individuals to wear masks in public places, which statement comes closer to your view, even if neither is exactly right?

Protecting personal liberty is more important, and requiring people to wear masks infringes on that

Protecting the common good is more important, and requiring people to wear masks is a matter of health or safety

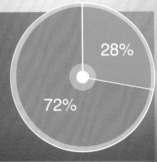

Source: "On COVID-19 Vaccine, Mask Requirements, Americans Prioritize Common Good Over Personal Liberty," *USA Today*/Ipsos. August 18, 2021. www.ipsos.com.

happens, patients with heart attacks, cancer, and other serious illnesses or injuries may not be able to get the care they need. This is another way in which one person's decision to not wear a mask or get vaccinated may harm others.

Protecting Vulnerable People

Pandemic-related mandates are also important to help protect people who cannot protect themselves. The ACLU is an organization that works to protect individual rights and promote freedom. Yet the organization supports pandemic-related mandates. Two directors at the ACLU, David Cole and Daniel Mach, explain that vaccine mandates "protect the most vulnerable among us, including people with disabilities and fragile immune systems, children too young to be vaccinated and communities of color hit hard by the disease."[17]

Very young children cannot keep a mask on and cannot get vaccinated. Some people with disabilities and health conditions cannot get vaccinated or face a greater risk of serious disease or death if they get infected. In Texas, schools are not allowed to mandate that children wear masks. Parents of children with disabilities filed a lawsuit arguing that the lack of mask mandates meant that their kids could not attend school safely.

Since a vaccine teaches a person's immune system to fight off a particular virus, vaccines do not work well for people with weak or impaired immune systems. As an example, Colin Powell, the former US secretary of state, passed away from COVID-19 in October 2021 at the age of eighty-four. He had been vaccinated, but a previous bout with cancer had left his immune system weakened. So, the vaccine did not work for him. Mandates can help prevent more unnecessary deaths such as this one.

In addition, mandates help protect certain populations of people who do not have control over the safety of their work or living environments. They may not have enough space to maintain social distancing or to isolate. They may be unable to work from home and may have to risk their health daily on public transportation or in crowded working or living environments. These issues are most common in low-income and marginalized communities, including many communities of color. If some people in these communities do not or cannot wear masks or get vaccinated, the entire group is at greater risk of disease or death.

Voluntary Vaccination Did Not Work

Unfortunately, voluntary vaccination programs did not reach enough people in the United States. By December 2021, only around 75 percent of the US population had received at least one shot. To reach herd immunity, or a point at which the virus cannot spread because so many people are protected, at least 80 to 90 percent of the population has to be vaccinated. "The choice of too many individuals to go unvaccinated has already resulted in the worsening of the pandemic and the COVID-19 virus itself,"[18] write medical ethics experts Matthew K. Wynia, Thomas D. Harter, and Jason T. Eberl. In 2021, the SARS-CoV-2 virus mutated into the far more contagious Delta and Omicron variants.

> "The choice of too many individuals to go unvaccinated has already resulted in the worsening of the pandemic and the COVID-19 virus itself."[18]
>
> —Matthew K. Wynia, Thomas D. Harter, and Jason T. Eberl, medical ethics experts

The only choice the United States has at this point is to issue mandates that include penalties for those who refuse to comply. "At this stage in the pandemic, we need to change our playbook. . . . And that's going to include vaccine mandates,"[19] says Rebecca Weintraub, a public health expert at Ariadne Labs. The federal government does not have the power to require that all citizens get vaccinated. However, President Biden has taken steps to protect the public by mandating vaccination for certain groups. Unfortunately, the courts have struck down some of these mandates. These decisions go against the recommendations of numerous public health and infectious disease experts.

Vaccine Mandates Succeeded

State and city governments are also stepping up to protect the public. In California, the vaccination rate among three hundred thousand employees at the health care company Kaiser Permanente jumped from 78 to 97 percent after the state mandated that all health care workers get the vaccine or get tested twice every week. "These mandates do move the needle quite a bit on employees' willingness to get vaccinated,"[20] Laura Boudreau, an economist and labor expert at Columbia University, told *U.S. News & World Report*.

Though people may threaten to quit when mandates are announced, very few follow through. According to research from the Kaiser Family Foundation, just 5 percent of adults had left their job because of a vaccine mandate. "Mandates, so far, seem to be be the most effective thing we have to overcome the vaccine hesitancy," says Bradley Pollock, a doctor and expert in public health at the University of California, Davis. "It's more than good; it's very good."[21]

> "Mandates, so far, seem to be the most effective thing we have to overcome the vaccine hesitancy. It's more than good; it's very good."[21]
>
> —Dr. Bradley Pollock, a public health expert at the University of California, Davis

The United States must do whatever it can to increase the COVID-19 vaccination rate. That may need to include some form of vaccine passport. In parts of Canada, proof of vaccination is required to enter restaurants, bars, and gyms. Economists at Simon Fraser University in British Columbia found that in the week after one of these mandates began, the number of first doses given increased by more than 60 percent.

In July 2021, the Yale School of Public Health estimated that COVID-19 vaccinations in the United States had saved 279,000 lives and prevented 1.25 million hospitalizations. That is a lot of suffering and death avoided. Unfortunately, avoidable infections are still happening. Mandates are society's best option to protect people and save lives.

Chapter Two

Have Lockdowns Been Worth the Economic and Social Harm?

Lockdowns Saved Lives and Communities Bounced Back

- Lockdowns greatly reduced the spread of COVID-19.
- Governments provided money and programs to support the economy.
- Schools and businesses came up with creative ways for learning and work to continue at home.

The Debate at a Glance

Lockdowns Did More Harm than Good

- Lockdowns benefited wealthy people and harmed poor people.
- Economies suffered greatly during lockdowns, and unemployment surged.
- Closed schools harmed children's development.
- Drug addiction, abuse, and mental health issues all escalated during lockdown.

Lockdowns Saved Lives and Communities Bounced Back

"I don't think any human endeavor has ever saved so many lives in such a short period of time. There have been huge personal costs to staying home and canceling events, but the data show that each day made a profound difference. By using science and cooperating, we changed the course of history."

—Solomon Hsiang, director of the Global Policy Laboratory at University of California, Berkeley

Quoted in Edward Lempinen, "Emergency COVID-19 Measures Prevented More than 500 Million Infections, Study Finds," Berkeley Public Policy: The Goldman School, June 8, 2020. https://gspp.berkeley.edu.

Consider these questions as you read:

1. Whereas China had extremely strict lockdowns, Sweden had almost no lockdown at all. Which approach do you think makes more sense and why?
2. What does "flattening the curve" mean and why is this important? How did lockdowns help with this?
3. How did lockdowns impact you and your family? What did your school do to help students learn during the pandemic? Do you think you had enough support? Explain your answer.

Editor's note: The discussion that follows presents common arguments made in support of this perspective, reinforced by facts, quotes, and examples taken from various sources.

At the beginning of 2020, gathering with other people was risky. Restaurants closed, sports teams stopped playing, and people canceled weddings, vacations, and other plans. Nothing like this had ever happened before. Still, most people accepted that lockdowns were a difficult but necessary sacrifice.

The more people stayed separated, the fewer people would sicken and die from COVID-19. Researchers at Imperial College London found that lockdown orders in Europe during the spring of 2020 saved an estimated 3.1 million lives. Samir Bhatt, an infectious disease expert and the study's coauthor, explained that "without any interventions, such as lockdown and school closures, there could have been many more deaths from COVID-19."[22] Lockdowns helped keep people safe.

Slowing the Spread of Disease

Before lockdown measures went into effect, the SARS-CoV-2 virus was spreading exponentially, with case numbers doubling every two days, according to Solomon Hsiang and a team at the University of California, Berkeley. Hsiang studied the effects of lockdown policies in China, France, Iran, Italy, South Korea, and the United States between January and April 2020. In June 2020 Hsiang said, "So many have suffered tragic losses already. And yet, April and May would have been even more devastating if we had done nothing, with a toll we probably can't imagine."[23]

Exponential growth means that each infection has a cascading effect. One infected person will likely infect several more, and then each of those people will likely pass the disease on to a number of people, and so on. A line representing this growth on a graph curves steadily upward toward a sharp peak. Preventing even a few infections can cancel out many, many more. On a line graph, prevention of infections results in an ascending line that levels out instead of increasing more sharply. So people called this "flattening the curve."[24] Lockdowns were one of the most effective ways to do this.

> "So many have suffered tragic losses already. And yet, April and May would have been even more devastating if we had done nothing, with a toll we probably can't imagine."[23]
>
> —Solomon Hsiang, director of the Global Policy Laboratory at the University of California, Berkeley

Safety Versus Freedom

Everywhere, officials in charge of imposing lockdowns had to find a balance between keeping people safe and allowing them freedom. China imposed one of the world's harshest lockdowns; consequently, it had relatively few COVID-19 cases or deaths. In some places, people were not allowed to leave their homes at all and had to order in all supplies. Lockdowns as strict as China's simply were not possible in many parts of the world, including the United States, where individual freedom is highly valued. However, even the looser restrictions imposed in the United States made a difference and helped slow the spread of disease. "I think lockdowns were necessary," Tom Inglesby, director of the Johns Hopkins Center for Health Security, said in May 2020. "They actually have changed the course of the epidemic in the United States."[25] He went on to say that the lockdowns had made it possible for states to start carefully re-opening during the summer of 2020.

Unlike almost every other country in the world, Sweden chose not to lockdown its population during the pandemic. Large public gatherings were banned, but schools stayed open, and so did restaurants, gyms, hair salons, movie theaters, and sporting events. The country gambled that if vulnerable people stayed home and enough healthy people got the disease and recovered, they might be able to weather the pandemic without too much economic harm done. Meanwhile, Sweden's neighbor Norway imposed lockdowns similar to the ones in the United States and most of the rest of the world.

> "I think lockdowns were necessary. They actually have changed the course of the epidemic in the United States."[25]
>
> —Tom Inglesby, director of the Johns Hopkins Center for Health Security

Sweden and Norway have very similar public health care systems, and their populations usually have a similar life expectancy. So, their different approaches to managing the pandemic prove how important lockdowns were. Sweden's gamble had a devastating result—a COVID-19 death rate ten times higher than Norway's. "They underestimated the mortality tremendously,"[26] Claudia Hanson of Sweden's Karolinska Institute told the website Business Insider. Nursing homes and elder care facilities suffered especially terrible losses. The king of Sweden, Carl XVI Gustaf, even admitted that his government had made the wrong choice. "I think we have failed," he said in December 2020. "We have a large number who have died and that is terrible. It is something we all suffer with."[27]

Easing Economic Burdens

Governments around the world understood that lockdowns would seriously harm their economies. However, some loss of jobs and income was the price they had to pay to avoid mass suffering and death during the pandemic. As people lost their jobs and businesses lost income, governments found ways to help.

In Australia, for example, the JobKeeper program provided money to businesses to help them stay open and pay their workers during the crisis. Australia's prime minister, Scott Morrison, called the program "a lifeline to not only get through this crisis, but bounce back together on the other side."[28] Many US states started similar programs to help local businesses remain open. The federal government also gave out Economic Impact Payments directly to over 90 million taxpayers.

In addition, the US government extended unemployment benefits and halted evictions during the spring and summer of 2020. People who had lost their jobs could continue to receive payments until it was safe to return to work. And those who could not pay their rent or their mortgage were allowed to stay in their homes. When the White House announced this program in 2020, Diane Yentel, chief executive officer (CEO) of the National Low Income Housing Coalition, said on National Public Radio, "It's a pretty extraordinary and bold and unprecedented measure that the White House is taking that will save lives and prevent tens of millions of people from losing their homes in the middle of a pandemic."[29]

As it became safe to lift lockdown orders, businesses bounced back and people returned to work. A September 2021 report

Sweden's Choice Not to Lockdown Had Dire Consequences

Sweden stayed mostly open during the pandemic. Germany, on the other hand, put strict lockdown rules into place. Comparing the strictness of a country's lockdown measures against the rate of growth of infections reveals that lockdowns had the power to slow the spread of the virus and prevent deaths.

Stringency of Measures and New Cases per Million

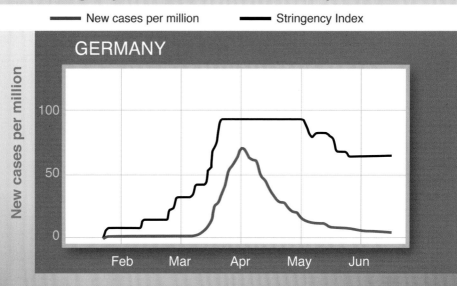

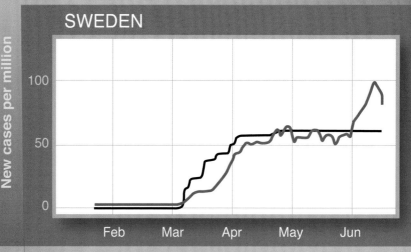

Note: The metrics used to calculate the Stringency Index include school closures; workplace closures; cancellation of public events; restrictions on public gatherings; closures of public transport; and stay-at-home requirements.

Source: Fabian Dablander. "Visualising The COVID-19 Pandemic." Science Versus Corona, June 17, 2020. https://scienceversuscorona.com.

from the Brookings Institution found that the US economy was recovering well, mainly thanks to financial relief programs. The number of Americans in poverty actually fell from 12 percent in 2019 to 9 percent in 2020.

Remote Work and School

Lockdowns prevented most people from going to work or school in person. However, this did not always mean that a person lost a job or stopped learning. People began using technologies such as Zoom to hold meetings or attend classes from home. Many businesses increased the flexibility of work hours, added more sick leave, or found other ways to support employees. According to a 2020 Aon survey, 57 percent of US businesses provided money or equipment to help employees set up home offices.

Schools faced incredible challenges during lockdowns. Yet many found creative ways to support their students. In Bridgeton, New Jersey, for example, the school system set up drive-through locations where families could pick up free or reduced-price school lunches. "We have so many barriers to kids learning. Nutrition should not be one of them,"[30] said Adele H. LaTourette, director of Hunger Free New Jersey. Some students do not have access to computers or the internet at home, so many schools sent devices home for kids to use. In Charleston, West Virginia, schools sent iPads to students' homes on buses that were already distributing school meals. These schools also helped get free internet service to some families. Sometimes, they sent out buses equipped with Wi-Fi hot spots.

Lockdowns were extremely difficult for everyone, but people found ways to cope. If lockdowns had not happened, even more people would likely have sickened and died. This could have led to widespread chaos. Recovery from the pandemic would have been even more difficult without lockdowns.

Lockdowns Did More Harm than Good

"Let's get back to work, let's get back to living. Let's be smart about it. Those of us who're 70-plus, we'll take care of ourselves. But don't sacrifice the country."

—Dan Patrick, lieutenant governor of Texas

Quoted in Ezra Klein, "The Debate over Ending Social Distancing to Save the Economy, Explained," Vox, March 27, 2020. www.vox.com.

Consider these questions as you read:

1. What do you think of the argument that the economic harms resulting from lockdowns may have been greater than the harm from more widespread COVID-19 infections? Explain.
2. What are "deaths of despair," and how did lockdowns make this type of death more likely?
3. What factors made it difficult or impossible for low-income and marginalized communities to follow lockdown orders?

Editor's note: The discussion that follows presents common arguments made in support of this perspective, reinforced by facts, quotes, and examples taken from various sources.

In early April 2020, over half of the world's population was under some form of lockdown order. People were told it was not safe to go to school or work or to travel to see family. Guo Jing, a social worker in Wuhan, China, experienced the world's first lockdown during January 2020. "The world is quiet, and the silence is horrifying," she wrote in her diary. "The government hasn't said how long the lockdown will last, nor how we can carry on functioning."[31]

Although lockdowns did prevent some amount of suffering and death from COVID-19, the costs of shutting down entire towns, cities, and countries were extreme. Lost jobs, untreated health conditions, closed schools, lack of social support, and other stressors also led to suffering and sometimes even death. A December 2021 poll by Scott Rasmussen of Ballotpedia found that 58 percent of Americans believed lockdowns did more harm than good. Plus, lockdowns did not stop the pandemic. The disease continued to spread, and new, even more contagious, variants emerged despite people's efforts to stay apart.

Economic Harm

Lockdowns caused an immense amount of economic harm. In the United States, the unemployment rate reached almost 15 percent, which was the highest rate recorded in the country since the Great Depression. Younger people, women, and people identifying as Black or Hispanic were more likely to lose their jobs or work fewer hours, according to a 2021 report from the Congressional Research Service.

Lockdowns could have been managed in a way that let most businesses continue to operate. For example, indoor dining probably should have been shut down, but schools, museums, and retail shops could have continued to function with safety measures, such as mask wearing, in place. "I think the positive effect of more commerce on employment probably would have outweighed the higher infection rates in most places,"[32] says Deborah Lucas, a professor of finance at the Sloan School of Management at the Massachusetts Institute of Technology (MIT).

> "I think the positive effect of more commerce on employment probably would have outweighed the higher infection rates in most places."[32]
>
> —Deborah Lucas, a professor at the MIT Sloan School of Management

Harm to Children

The closing of schools, especially, was unjustifiable. Children were not at high risk of getting sick or dying from COVID-19, but missing school posed a huge risk to their welfare. Schools offer not only education but also a safe space with social support and regular meals. Researchers have linked closed schools to many alarming problems for kids and teens: less social interaction, less physical activity, more mental health problems, and more exposure to abusive, chaotic, or neglectful home environments. Virtual schooling was not a good replacement for in-person learning, especially among younger children. Many families did not have the time, technology, or resources to support children's learning at home.

In addition, research has shown that schools do not contribute in a major way to the spread of COVID-19. A study from October 2021 found that schools could reopen for in-person learning without a substantial increase in the number of COVID-19 cases in the community, as long as the schools and their communities were following safety measures such as mask wearing.

Deaths of Despair

The pandemic itself was stressful. Lockdowns compounded this stress by isolating people and putting many out of work. In 2019, one in ten adults reported symptoms of anxiety or depression. This jumped to four in ten during 2020, according to the US Census Bureau's Household Pulse Survey. Domestic violence also increased. Lost jobs and other stressors meant partners had more things to worry about and argue about. Also, abusers and victims could not easily separate. "Those fleeing abuse may not have a place to get away from abusive partners,"[33] explains Clare Cannon, a social and environmental justice expert at the University of California, Davis.

An estimated one hundred thousand Americans died of drug overdoses in 2020, a spike of 30 percent over the previous year. Karen Butcher's son Matthew died of an overdose in 2020, after the restaurant where he worked as a bartender had shut down. "He was lonely. He was depressed. He didn't have a reason any more to get up and keep going,"[34] Butcher says. Suicides and alcohol-related deaths also increased. Economist Anne Case of Princeton named these "deaths of despair."[35] Before the pandemic struck, Case had discovered that economic

Lockdowns Sent the US Economy into a Crisis

During the height of lockdowns in the US in April 2020, unemployment skyrocketed to 14.7%. The impacts were uneven, though. Certain groups of people lost their jobs at much high rates than others. Financial hardship is linked to higher rates of mental illness, poverty, drug addiction, domestic abuse, and death.

The unemployment rate for Black Americans	16.7%
The unemployment rate for Hispanic Americans	18.9%
The unemployment rate for people working in restaurants, hotels, event planning	39.8%
The unemployment rate for low-wage workers	40%

Source: Lauren Aratani. "Jobless America: The Coronavirus Unemployment Crisis in Figures." *The Guardian* (Manchester, UK), May 28, 2020. www.theguardian.com.

troubles are the main cause for this type of death. Lockdowns increased economic hardship and also took away people's social outlets.

Lockdowns created the perfect storm for deaths of despair. During the first few weeks of the pandemic in the United States, death counts were higher than normal by 15,400. Of these excess deaths, just 8,128 were attributed to COVID-19, according to research by the Yale School of Public Health. A portion of the rest were deaths of despair.

Unequal Protection

Worst of all, lockdowns did not stop the spread of COVID-19. In a 2021 study, researchers from the University of Chicago's Harris

School of Public Policy found that the US states with the strictest lockdowns did not experience fewer infections or deaths than states with loose lockdowns. The researchers say the reason for this is likely that people made their own decisions over whether or not to follow the orders. Some chose not to lockdown or could not lockdown.

In wealthy communities, most people had private space where they could easily remain separate from others. Many had access to technology so they could work or attend school or consult with a doctor or order groceries from home. They had their own cars so they could move around safely. Many people living in impoverished and marginalized communities had none of these things. "Sheltering in place is a luxury that most of the developing world cannot afford,"[36] writes Julian C. Jamison, an economics expert at the University of Exeter, in the *Washington Post*.

> "We believe that lockdowns kill people through disruption of health services and deprivation of livelihoods."[37]
>
> —A group of health experts, writing for the medical journal, the *Lancet*

Anyone in a shared living space could not safely separate from others at home. Many low-income workers, including line cooks, nannies, store clerks, nurse's aides, and farmworkers, also could not work from home. If they lost their jobs, they may not have been able to feed their families or stay in their homes. "We believe that lockdowns kill people through disruption of health services and deprivation of livelihoods,"[37] write a group of health experts in the medical journal the *Lancet*.

Although essential workers were hailed as heroes around the world, they often felt forced to sacrifice their safety to support the safety of others. "I have a problem with all this hero talk," admitted Karleigh Frisbie Brogan, a grocery store cashier in Portland, Oregon. "Cashiers and shelf-stockers and delivery-truck drivers aren't heroes. They're victims. To call them heroes is to justify their exploitation."[38]

A Lesson from South Korea

South Korea managed to weather the pandemic without a lockdown and also without very many infections or deaths. Instead, the country aggressively tested, traced, and isolated. In early March 2020, the country was testing twenty thousand people every day, more than anywhere else in the world. And results were coming back within one day thanks to a network of labs set up for this purpose. Those who showed symptoms were sent to quarantine centers. This helped the country keep the virus from spreading out of control without any lockdowns.

Lockdowns were ineffective and harmful, especially to underprivileged populations. They were like giant hammers trying to squash the virus, which was like a swarm of tiny, deadly insects. Yes, some of the insects were smashed, but the hammers damaged too many other things as well. The pandemic could have been managed effectively without completely shutting down borders, businesses, and schools.

Chapter Three

Has Vaccine Distribution Failed?

Vaccine Distribution Has Failed

- Wealthy countries have hoarded vaccines, preventing other countries from obtaining them.
- Outreach efforts have not succeeded in many low-income communities in the United States.
- Anti-vaccination (anti-vax) movements have spread fear and misinformation, hindering vaccination campaigns.

The Debate at a Glance

Vaccines Reached Billions and Saved Lives

- Researchers worldwide cooperated to develop vaccines remarkably quickly and efficiently.
- Vaccines were made available to anyone for free in many countries, including the United States.
- Vaccinated people are well protected from severe illness, even when new variants and breakthrough infections occur.

Vaccine Distribution Has Failed

"The inequitable distribution of vaccines has been a failure for humanity."

—Tedros Adhanom Ghebreyesus, director general of WHO

Quoted in VOA News, "WHO Chief: Inequitable Vaccine Distribution Is 'Failure for Humanity,'" December 18, 2021. www.voanews.com.

Consider these questions as you read:

1. What do you think about reports that wealthy countries hoarded vaccines? Should they have acted differently? Explain.
2. In what ways was vaccine distribution within the United States unfair? What barriers prevented some people from getting their shots?
3. Give two examples of harmful misinformation about the COVID-19 vaccines and how this information can be checked for accuracy.

Editor's note: The discussion that follows presents common arguments made in support of this perspective, reinforced by facts, quotes, and examples taken from various sources.

"Every American who wants the vaccine will be able to get the vaccine. . . . It will end the pandemic."[39] President Donald Trump made this bold prediction in December 2020. Unfortunately, he was wrong. The pandemic did not end because not enough people received vaccines. As of January 2022, approximately half of the world's population and 62 percent of the US population was fully vaccinated against COVID-19. This was not good enough to stop the pandemic.

Even though vaccines had been available for an entire year in January 2022, the pandemic was surging yet again in the United States. COVID-19 hospitalizations were even higher than they had been one year earlier, when vaccines were not yet widely available. "A year ago, we all hoped that by now vaccines would be helping us all emerge from the long, dark tunnel of the pandemic. Instead, as we enter the third year of the pandemic, the death toll has more than tripled, and the world remains in its grip,"[40] said Tedros Adhanom Ghebreyesus, director-general of WHO, in December 2021. Vaccine distribution had failed.

Unfair Distribution

While vaccines were still being developed, experts made plans for how to give them out fairly. The program COVAX was supposed to make sure that those most vulnerable to infection or most at risk of death would get vaccinated first, no matter where they lived. Health care workers, people over the age of sixty-five, and people with health conditions that put them at greater risk of death from COVID-19 were supposed to be first in line.

This is not what actually happened. "The systems that have been set up to vaccinate the world have failed utterly,"[41] says Achal Prabhala, a science writer based in Bengaluru, India. Most wealthy countries vaccinated vulnerable people first, then began vaccinating the rest of their populations instead of sharing doses with other countries that needed them. In April 2021, Melissa Mahtani was eligible to get vaccinated because she lives in the United Kingdom, but her parents—who were at a higher risk due to their age—lived in Zambia, Africa. They had no doses available to them. "I felt racked with guilt over being eligible to get a vaccine when they couldn't,"[42] she says.

> "The systems that have been set up to vaccinate the world have failed utterly."[41]
>
> —Achal Prabhala, science writer

Wealthy countries, including Canada, the United Kingdom, and the United States, had ordered far more doses than they needed, long before any vaccines were approved for use. The United Kingdom ordered enough for four times its population, and Canada for five times its population, according to data from Duke University. "Rich countries are hoarding the vaccine supply,"[43] said Niko Lusiani of Oxfam in December 2020. As a result, young, healthy adults in the United States got booster shots before vulnerable people in many other parts of the world had received even one shot. As of July 2021, 84 percent of all vaccine doses had gone to high- and middle-income

countries. Low-income countries had given out just 0.3 percent of all doses. "We cannot accept that in a world where the technology exists to save lives, we let people die because they live in poor countries,"[44] says Ngozi Okonjo-Iweala, director-general of the World Trade Organization.

Unequal Access

Even in the United States, where vaccines were widely available for free, not everyone who wanted a shot was able to get one. Black and Hispanic communities were hit much harder by the pandemic than White communities but received far fewer vaccinations, especially early on. Black people make up 13 percent of the US population but had only received 8.3 percent of vaccinations as of April 1, 2021, according to data from the Association of American Medical Colleges. For Hispanic people, these percentages were 18 percent and 9.5 percent, respectively. All too often, people in these communities had more difficulty accessing vaccination appointments.

In Massachusetts, for example, mass vaccination sites were set up at sports arenas and convention centers. To get vaccinated, a person had to sign up online and then get to the appointment. If someone did not have a device with an internet connection or were not internet savvy, they could not secure an appointment. If they had a disability, could not take time off work, or lacked a car, they might not be able to get there. Black, Hispanic, and low-income communities were more likely to face these sorts of barriers. Many cities did set up clinics in low-income communi-

Wealthy Countries Hoarded the Vaccine Supply

As of December 2021, an average of 83 percent of the eligible people in high-income countries had received at least one shot to protect them from COVID-19, while in low-income countries the average was just 21 percent. This chart shows the number of doses given out per 100 people. (The numbers are 200 or higher in some countries because one person may have received as many as two doses plus a booster shot).

Global Vaccine Distribution

0   20   40   60   80   100   120   140   160   180   200   220   260   280

Source: Smriti Mallapaty et al., "How COVID Vaccines Shaped 2021 in Eight Powerful Charts," *Nature News*, December 16, 2021. www.nature.com.

ties of color, but people from wealthier white communities often grabbed all the appointments.

Systemic racism also affected the willingness of people of color in the United States to get vaccinated. Doctors and medical researchers have repeatedly failed, mistreated, or even abused people of color in the United States. It is understandable that they would be reluctant to trust this system. Sandra Lindsay, a nurse at Long Island Jewish Medical Center in New York City was the first

American to receive a COVID-19 vaccine. She is Black and hoped her choice might ease some people's fears. But she knew it was not enough. "I know just me getting the vaccine won't erase the centuries of mistrust and any inhumane and harmful behaviors that have taken place,"[45] Lindsay says. Public health officials should have worked more closely with spokespeople from within these communities to help ease people's fears and reduce distrust.

Opposition of the Anti-Vax Movement

A fear of COVID-19 vaccination circulated among many Americans, not only those dealing with a history of medical injustice. Much of the fear was fueled by a decades-old anti-vax movement. People who were already against vaccination immediately began spreading rumors and misinformation about COVID-19 vaccines.

Many of the rumors warned of harmful side effects. Vaccines do have some side effects, but dangerous ones are extremely rare. Others worried that the vaccines were too experimental since they were developed so quickly. In fact, the vaccines went through very rigorous testing. People also spread rumors that vaccines were altering deoxyribonucleic acid (DNA), contained microchips, or caused infertility. "These claims are false, dangerous and deeply irresponsible,"[46] said a spokesperson for the Department of Health & Social Care in the United Kingdom.

False claims and fears about the COVID-19 vaccines were especially common among conservative communities in the United States. An October 2021 survey by the Brookings Institution found that 90 percent of Democrats had been vaccinated compared to just 58 percent of Republicans. "We find a huge correlation between belief in misinformation and being unvaccinated,"[47] says Liz Hamel of the Kaiser Family Foundation. Even if people did not believe the rumors and misinformation, they might still feel confused or doubtful and might hesitate to get vaccinated. Everett Jiles of Front Royal, Virginia, describes himself as a Christian conservative. He did not want the vaccine at first.

"You had all these different views being pushed and no idea who to believe," he said. "It just felt wrong, so I was against it."[48] Then Jiles got COVID-19 in July 2021 and nearly died. He started telling friends to get the vaccine. Unfortunately, it is already too late for some. The Kaiser Family Foundation estimates that 163,000 COVID-19 deaths between June and December 2021 in the United States could have been prevented if people had gotten vaccinated sooner.

Low Vaccination Rates Put Everyone in Danger

Vaccine inequality and low rates of vaccination are very dangerous. "Any country that has surges of covid infections combined with very low vaccination rates is a potential hotspot of some new horror, some new variant,"[49] says Prabhala. This has already happened twice with Delta and Omicron, which rapidly spread around the world. New variants have even sickened vaccinated people. Breakthrough infections tend to be less severe but can still kill. Many have died who did not have to die. Unless the world finds a way to get vaccines to all countries and all people, we "risk condemning the world to an endless pandemic,"[50] explains Nick Dearden, director of the UK-based social justice organization Global Justice Now.

Vaccines Reached Billions and Saved Lives

"The COVID-19 vaccines are a marvel of modern science. . . . They're doing what they promised, that is saving lives, offering very high protection against severe illness and death. In some countries, the death toll would have been double what it is now without the vaccines."

—Hans Henri P. Kluge, WHO regional director for Europe

Quoted in European Centre for Disease Prevention and Control, "WHO/ECDC: Nearly Half a Million Lives Saved by COVID-19 Vaccination in Less than a Year," November 25, 2021. www.ecdc.europa.eu.

Consider these questions as you read:

1. What factors helped scientists develop and test vaccines against COVID-19 extremely quickly?
2. What strategy would you use if you were trying to persuade a group of reluctant people to get vaccinated?
3. Do you think COVID-19 vaccines will end the pandemic? Why or why not?

Editor's note: The discussion that follows presents common arguments made in support of this perspective, reinforced by facts, quotes, and examples taken from various sources.

In less than a year, humanity developed and distributed highly effective vaccines against COVID-19. This was a triumph for the entire world. Never before had medical science worked so quickly and so cooperatively to find a solution to a problem. Without COVID-19 vaccines, an estimated 1.1 million more people would have died in 2021—and that is just in the United States. Vaccines also prevented an estimated 10.3 million hospitalizations in the United States, according to research by the Commonwealth Fund. "The vaccines have had a huge impact on averting deaths and helping [countries'] economies return to normal,"[51] says Soumya Swaminathan, chief scientist at WHO.

There have been problems with vaccine distribution, but experts have been working hard to find solutions. The fact that so many have been vaccinated so quickly is still a remarkable feat. As of January 2022, half of the world's population, or almost 4 billion people, were fully vaccinated against COVID-19. Tens of millions of doses were still being given out every day, meaning this number will only grow.

Science to the Rescue

Before this pandemic, it typically took around ten years to get a new vaccine ready and approved for use. The first COVID-19 vaccines were given out just 332 days after scientists first identified and described SARS-CoV-2. "This is an unprecedented success. To go from isolating a new virus to having a vaccine approved by the FDA . . . in less than a year, is simply something we have never seen before,"[52] comments Dr. Carlos del Rio of the Emory University School of Medicine.

This lightning-fast development happened without cutting any corners. The vaccines went through all the necessary safety tests and clinical trials. "The speed is a reflection of years of work that went before,"[53] explains Dr. Anthony Fauci, chief medical adviser to the US president and director of the National Institute of Allergy and Infectious Diseases. Scientists already understood coronaviruses very well and had already been developing new vaccine technologies.

Faced with a worldwide crisis, scientists and medical researchers worked around the clock. "We had to reduce the timelines. So we came up with a number of really innovative strategies,"[54] remarks Ugur Sahin, CEO of BioNTech, the company that worked with Pfizer to develop one of the first COVID-19 vaccines. BioNTech set up shifts that ran through evenings and weekends. It also ran tests in parallel instead of one after another. "It shows how fast vaccine development can proceed when there is a true global emergency and sufficient resources,"[55] observes Dan Barouch, director of the Center for Virology and Vaccine Research at Harvard Medical School.

Creating and testing vaccines was only one part of the challenge. Companies and governments also found ways to manufacture billions of doses. As of December 2021, 10 billion doses had been given out. "Just making that much vaccine has been the standout success,"[56] says Gagandeep Kang, a virologist at Christian Medical College in Vellore, India.

The Joy of Reconnection

Vaccines may not have ended the pandemic, but they have made a huge difference in helping the world heal. In the early days of the pandemic, things seemed hopeless and terrifying. "I saw firsthand the devastation that the virus caused in hospitals," says Dr. Celine Gounder of the Grossman School of Medicine at New York University. "We were overwhelmed. Patients were dying. I walked by mortuary trucks parked near the hospital on the way to work."[57] No one knew how soon vaccines might be available or how well they might work.

In the end, vaccines were ready sooner than anyone expected, and they worked better than expected too. Sahin had hoped the vaccine might prevent severe illness in 70 to 80 percent of people. In fact, it worked much better than that. Over 90 percent of people were well protected by the vaccine. "This was incredible. This was just breathtaking," he said. "In this moment we understood, there's a vaccine for mankind. Corona is a problem that can be solved."[58]

> "This was incredible. This was just breathtaking. In this moment we understood, there's a vaccine for mankind. Corona is a problem that can be solved."[58]
>
> —Ugur Sahin, CEO of BioNTech

As people began getting their shots, they experienced the joys of reconnection. They hugged their mom and dad or grandma and grandpa for the first time in over a year. They met babies that had been born during the pandemic. They gathered for memorial services or weddings. Nassim Assefi is a doctor based at the Lummi Tribal Health Center in Bellingham, Washington. Her sister got married in a small ceremony for immediate family after everyone had been vaccinated. "It was so special to celebrate, cook, and hug each other indoors and unmasked," says Assefi. "It was at once strangely normal and also like a precious longed-for gift that I, for one, will never take for granted again."[59]

Convincing the Reluctant

Governments and organizations around the world helped pay for the development and distribution of COVID-19 vaccines. In Australia, China, Japan, the United States, and many other countries, shots were given for free to anybody who qualified. In most places, health care workers, people ages sixty-five and older, and people with health conditions that put them at a high risk could get their shots first. By the end of spring 2021, the United States had doses available for any adult who wanted one. Shots for kids became available later in the year.

From the beginning, public health experts understood that getting the vaccines out to everyone would not be easy. Many US cities launched programs that aimed to bring the vaccines into low-income communities and communities of color. People in those communities had been especially hard hit by the pandemic, but many had not been able to get vaccinated or were not sure whether it was safe. Pierre Sandoval worked as a canvasser for Community Coalition, an organization working to improve social and economic conditions in Los Angeles. He knocked on doors in predominantly Black and Hispanic neighborhoods of the city to

The Global Vaccination Campaign Is Going Strong

The world has never before produced and administered so many vaccines in such a short time span. Though the rollout has been uneven, the number of vaccinated people continues to rise worldwide. An average of 23 million doses were being given out daily in February 2022.

Rate of Global Vaccination Campaign

As of end of February 2022, the global 7-day moving average of administered doses is about 23 million per day.

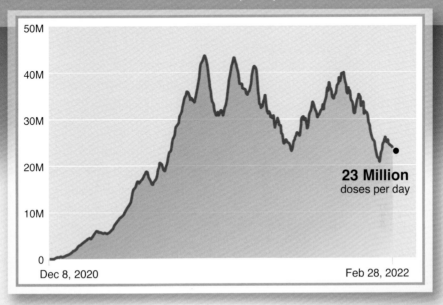

23 Million
doses per day

Dec 8, 2020   Feb 28, 2022

Source: Henrik Pettersson et al., "Tracking Covid-19 Vaccinations Worldwide," CNN, February 28, 2022. www.cnn.com.

help encourage people to get vaccinated. He got a lot of questions. "They're not used to free healthcare. . . . Our people are like, is this real? Is this something I can trust?"[60] he said.

These types of programs are especially helpful when the people offering vaccine information or appointments come from the same background as those in the selected community. This worked especially well in Indigenous communities, which wound up having the highest vaccination rate of any racial or ethnic group in the United States. Many tribes used native-language speakers or elders to help spread the word about vaccination. They also brought the vaccine directly to people who needed it. Kathleen Adams, a nurse at the Fort Belknap reservation in Montana, carried a cooler filled with vaccines on her shoulder. "She'll see somebody across the road and run over and start to persuade them to get vaccinated,"[61] says Richard Read, a *Los Angeles Times* journalist who reported on such efforts.

Vaccinating the World

The COVAX program was set up to help get vaccines to low-income countries. Though the program has not worked as well as many hoped, by January 2022 COVAX had supplied 1 billion doses of COVID-19 vaccines to Bangladesh, Brazil, Ethiopia, Fiji, Ghana, and other countries, and more doses were on the way.

It turned out that vaccination could not completely prevent COVID-19. Breakthrough infections were possible, especially when new variants of the disease began to circulate. However, when vaccinated people got sick, they were much less likely than unvaccinated people to die or require hospitalization. Widespread vaccination is still the world's best bet to end the pandemic and save lives.

Source Notes

Overview: The COVID-19 Pandemic

1. Quoted in Aaron Mesmer, "Mother of 8 Nearly Killed by COVID-19 Warns Others Who Are Hesitant to Get Vaccinated," Fox 13, July 26, 2021. www.fox13news.com.
2. World Health Organization, "WHO Director-General's Opening Remarks at the Media Briefing on COVID-19—11 March 2020," March 11, 2020. www.who.int.

Chapter One: Do Pandemic Mandates Violate Individual Rights?

3. Quoted in Emily Stewart, "Anti-Maskers Explain Themselves," Vox, August 7, 2020. www.vox.com.
4. Quoted in Nathan S. Chapman and Kenji Yoshino, "The Fourteenth Amendment Due Process Clause," National Constitution Center, 2021. https://constitutioncenter.org.
5. Quoted in FindLaw, Washington v. Harper. https://caselaw.findlaw.com.
6. Quoted in Amy Kawata, "'Thought It Was My Body, My Choice': Northrop Grumman Employees Protest Vaccine Mandate," CBS Baltimore, October 18, 2021. https://baltimore.cbslocal.com.
7. Quoted in Kawata, "'Thought It Was My Body, My Choice.'"
8. Quoted in Kawata, "'Thought It Was My Body, My Choice.'"
9. Quoted in Kawata, "'Thought It Was My Body, My Choice.'"
10. Elise Stefanik, "Stefanik Slams Biden for Forcing Vaccine Mandate on Private Businesses," US House of Representatives, November 4, 2021. https://stefanik.house.gov.
11. Jim Banks (@RepJimBanks), "Vaccine mandates are unAmerican!," Twitter, September 12, 2021. https://twitter.com/repjimbanks/status/1437159474846896130?lang=ar.
12. Quoted in Andrea Hsu, "Thousands of Workers Are Opting to Get Fired, Rather than Take the Vaccine," Morning Edition, National Public Radio, October 24, 2021. www.npr.org.
13. Quoted in Sarah Maslin Nir, "Their Jobs Made Them Get Vaccinated. They Refused," New York Times, October 24, 2021. www.nytimes.com.
14. Quoted in Eric Katz, "Meet the Federal Employees Who Will Refuse the COVID-19 Vaccine," Government Executive, October 18, 2021. www.govexec.com.

15. Quoted in Celine Gounder, "The Privilege of Immunity/Kathryn Olivarius, Juanita Mora, Esha Bhandari," *Epidemic* (podcast), season 1, episode 33, July 7, 2020. www.justhumanproductions.org.
16. Joe Biden, "Remarks by President Biden on Fighting the COVID-19 Pandemic," White House Briefing Room, September 9, 2021. www.whitehouse.gov.
17. David Cole and Daniel Mach, "We Work at the A.C.L.U. Here's What We Think About Vaccine Mandates," *New York Times*, September 2, 2021. www.nytimes.com.
18. Matthew K. Wynia, Thomas D. Harter, and Jason T. Eberl, "Why a Universal COVID-19 Vaccine Mandate Is Ethical Today," Health Affairs Forefront, November 3, 2021. www.healthaffairs.org.
19. Quoted in Isaac Chotiner, "How the Delta Variant Is Changing the Public-Health Playbook," *New Yorker,* August 3, 2021. www.hsph.harvard.edu.
20. Quoted in Mae Anderson and David Koenig, "Employer Vaccine Mandates Convert Some Workers, but Not All," *U.S. News & World Report*, September 28, 2021. www.usnews.com.
21. Quoted in Tommy Beer, "Covid-19 Vaccine Mandates Are Working—Here's the Proof," *Forbes,* October 4, 2021. www.forbes.com.

Chapter Two: Have Lockdowns Been Worth the Economic and Social Harm?

22. Quoted in Kate Wighton, "Lockdown and School Closures in Europe May Have Prevented 3.1m Deaths," Imperial College London, June 8, 2020. www.imperial.ac.uk.
23. Quoted in Edward Lempinen, "Emergency COVID-19 Measures Prevented More than 500 Million Infections, Study Finds," Berkeley Public Policy: The Goldman School, June 8, 2020. https://gspp.berkeley.edu.
24. Cathy Cassata, "Yes, Lockdowns Do Help Slow the Spread of COVID-19," Healthline, April 1, 2021. www.healthline.com.
25. Quoted in NBC News, "Full Inglesby: Total Deaths Depend 'On What People Decide to Do, Their Own Actions,'" *Meet the Press*, May 17, 2020. www.nbcnews.com.
26. Quoted in Aria Bendix, "A Year and a Half After Sweden Decided Not to Lock down, Its COVID-19 Death Rate Is Up to 10 Times Higher than Its Neighbors," Business Insider, August 21, 2021. www.businessinsider.com.
27. Quoted in Melissa Heikkillä, "Swedish King: Country Has 'Failed' on Coronavirus Pandemic," *Politico*, December 17, 2020. www.politico.eu.
28. Prime Minister of Australia, "$130 Billion JobKeeper Payment to Keep Australians in a Job," March 30, 2020. www.pm.gov.au.

29. Quoted in Chris Arnold, "CDC Issues Sweeping Temporary Halt on Evictions Nationwide Amid Pandemic," *Morning Edition,* National Public Radio, September 1, 2020. www.npr.org.
30. Quoted in Melanie Burney and Kristen A. Graham, "Meeting the Need: Schools Find Ways to Serve Up Meals for Kids amid the Pandemic," *Philadelphia Inquirer*, January 17, 2021. www.inquirer.com.
31. Quoted in Grace Tsoi, "Coronavirus Wuhan Diary: Living Alone in a City Gone Quiet," BBC, January 30, 2020. www.bbc.com.
32. Quoted in Neil Paine, "Experts Think the Economy Would Be Stronger If COVID-19 Lockdowns Had Been More Aggressive," FiveThirtyEight, September 22, 2020. https://fivethirtyeight.com.
33. Quoted in Karen Nikos-Rose, "COVID-19 Isolation Linked to Increased Domestic Violence, Researchers Suggest," University of California, Davis, February 24, 2021. www.ucdavis.edu.
34. Quoted in Scott Horsley, "They Lost Sons to Drug Overdoses: How the Pandemic May Be Fueling Deaths of Despair," *Morning Edition*, National Public Radio, January 26, 2021. www.npr.org.
35. Quoted in David Introcaso, "Deaths of Despair: The Unrecognized Tragedy of Working Class Immiseration," Stat, December 29, 2021. www.statnews.com.
36. Julian C. Jamison, "Lockdowns Will Starve People in Low-Income Countries," *Washington Post,* April 20, 2020. www.washingtonpost.com.
37. Damian Walker et al., "Lockdown Is Not Egalitarian: The Costs Fall on the Global Poor," *the Lancet,* June 19, 2020. www.thelancet.com.
38. Karleigh Frisbie Brogan, "Calling Me a Hero Only Makes You Feel Better," *The Atlantic,* April 18, 2020. www.theatlantic.com.

Chapter Three: Has Vaccine Distribution Failed?

39. Donald Trump, "Remarks by President Trump at the Operation Warp Speed Vaccine Summit," White House, December 8, 2020. https://trumpwhitehouse.archives.gov.
40. Quoted in VOA News, "WHO Chief: Inequitable Vaccine Distribution Is 'Failure for Humanity,'" December 18, 2021. www.voanews.com.
41. Quoted in Ayeisha Thomas-Smith, "Closing the Covid-19 Vaccination Gap," *Weekly Economics Podcast*, November 29, 2021. https://neweconomics.org.
42. Melissa Mahtani, "I Got Vaccinated—but My Family Can't, and the Guilt Is Killing Me," CNN, April 19, 2021. www.cnn.com.
43. Quoted in Michaeleen Doucleff, "How Rich Countries Are 'Hoarding' the World's Vaccines, in Charts," *Goats and Soda* (blog), National Public Radio, December 3, 2020. www.npr.org.
44. Ngozi Okonjo-Iweala, "DG Okonjo-Iweala: Vaccine Policy Key to Sustainable Economic and Trade Recovery," World Trade Organization, September 23, 2021. www.wto.org.

45. Quoted in Javonte Anderson, "America Has a History of Medically Abusing Black People. No Wonder Many Are Wary of COVID-19 Vaccines," *USA Today,* February 16, 2021. www.usatoday.com.
46. Quoted in Steve Stecklow and Andrew Macaskill, "The Ex-Pfizer Scientist Who Became an Anti-Vax Hero," Reuters, March 18, 2021. www.reuters.com.
47. Quoted in Geoff Brumfiel, "Inside the Growing Alliance Between Anti-Vaccine Activists and Pro-Trump Republicans," *All Things Considered*, National Public Radio, December 6, 2021. www.npr.org.
48. Quoted in Beth Howard, "Talking to Vaccine Skeptics in Rural, Conservative America," Association of American Medical Colleges, December 21, 2021. www.aamc.org.
49. Quoted in Thomas-Smith, "Closing the Covid-19 Vaccination Gap."
50. Quoted in Amnesty International, "G20's Bitter Divide on Global Vaccine Inequality Could Condemn World to an 'Endless Pandemic,' Charities Warn," October 30, 2021. www.amnesty.org.
51. Quoted in Smriti Mallapaty et al., "How COVID Vaccines Shaped 2021 in Eight Powerful Charts," *Nature,* December 16, 2021. www.nature.com.
52. Quoted in Ellen Eldridge, "COVID-19 Vaccines' Development an 'Unprecedented Success,' Emory Says," GPB News, Georgia Public Broadcasting, December 1, 2020. www.gpb.org.
53. Quoted in Lauran Neergard, "Years of Research Laid Groundwork for Speedy COVID-19 Shots," AP News, December 7, 2020. https://apnews.com.
54. Quoted in Kristen V. Brown, "Part Seven: The Vaccine Race," *Prognosis: Breakthrough* (podcast), Bloomberg, November 30, 2021. https://podcasts.apple.com.
55. Quoted in Philip Ball, "The Lightning-Fast Quest for COVID Vaccines—and What It Means for Other Diseases," *Nature,* December 18, 2020. www.nature.com.
56. Quoted in Mallapaty et al., "How COVID Vaccines Shaped 2021 in Eight Powerful Charts."
57. Celine Gounder, "Vaccine Joy/Andy Slavitt & Celine Gounder," *Epidemic* (podcast), season 1, episode 80, June 24, 2021. www.justhumanproductions.org.
58. Quoted in Brown. "Part Seven."
59. Quoted in Gounder, "Vaccine Joy."
60. Quoted in Erika D. Smith, "The Fight to Change COVID-19 Vaccine-Hesitant Hearts and Minds," *The Times* (podcast), *Los Angeles Times,* June 11, 2021. www.latimes.com.
61. Quoted in Erika D. Smith, "How Native Americans Became a Vaccine Success Story," *The Times* (podcast), *Los Angeles Times,* September 2, 2021. www.latimes.com.

COVID-19 Pandemic Facts

How the Pandemic Started

- The first cases of COVID-19 emerged in Wuhan, China, during December 2019.
- The coronavirus SARS-CoV-2 causes the disease COVID-19.
- Most scientists agreed that SARS-CoV-2 most likely arose naturally, when a disease that could only infect animals mutated and began infecting humans.
- The first confirmed case of COVID-19 in the United States was a man from Washington State who was tested on January 18, 2020.
- WHO declared a pandemic on March 11, 2020.

The Impact of the Pandemic

- Over 5.7 million people had died worldwide from COVID-19 as of February 2022, according to *Our World in Data*.
- The United States has had more confirmed cases and deaths than any other country worldwide, according to Statista.
- During 2020, one in three Americans caught COVID-19, according to a study published in *Nature*.
- Life expectancy in the United States dropped from 78.8 years in 2019 down to 77 years in 2020, according to the CDC.
- In December 2020 and January 2021, COVID-19 was the leading cause of death in the United States, passing cancer and heart disease, according to the Kaiser Family Foundation.

COVID-19 Disease and Prevention

- COVID-19 symptoms include fever, chills, cough, shortness of breath, tiredness, body aches, headache, loss of taste or smell, sore throat, congestion, nausea, and diarrhea.
- An infected person who has no symptoms can still spread the virus to others. It spreads through the air when an infected person coughs, sneezes, talks, or sings.
- Anyone may get seriously sick or die of COVID-19, though the risk is greater for elderly people or people with certain health conditions.

- Most COVID-19 vaccines require two doses. A booster shot six months after the second dose offers additional protection.
- The CDC recommends getting vaccinated to protect oneself and others. Wearing a mask in public, handwashing, checking for symptoms, and getting tested regularly can also help.

COVID-19 Vaccine Myths Busted

- COVID-19 vaccines cannot make a person sick with COVID-19 or shed the virus because these vaccines do not contain any virus. They contain instructions that tell the body how to defend itself against the virus.
- The ingredients in the COVID-19 vaccines are not dangerous. All of the vaccines went through extensive safety testing before being approved.
- A person who has had COVID-19 should still get vaccinated. A 2021 CDC study found that people who had recovered from COVID-19 and did not get vaccinated were two times as likely to get COVID-19 again.
- New variants of SARS-CoV-2 occur naturally as the original virus mutates. Vaccines may not be as effective against all variants, but they help reduce the spread of the virus, which lowers its chances of mutating.
- COVID-19 vaccines do not contain microchips, make people magnetic, alter DNA, or cause infertility. These harmful rumors have no foundation in scientific fact.

Related Organizations and Websites

Centers for Disease Control and Prevention (CDC)
www.cdc.gov
The CDC is the US government agency responsible for protecting the health of Americans. It is the source of up-to-date guidelines, scientific research, and information on all things related to the COVID-19 pandemic in the United States.

Coalition for Epidemic Preparedness Innovations (CEPI)
https://cepi.net
An international organization, CEPI was launched in 2017 with the goal of developing vaccines that could help the world respond to future epidemics and pandemics.

COVAX
www.who.int/initiatives/act-accelerator/covax
COVAX is a project managed by WHO, along with partner organizations CEPI, Gavi, and the United Nations Children's Fund, to help distribute COVID-19 vaccines fairly among the countries of the world. Its motto is, "With a fast-moving pandemic, no one is safe, unless everyone is safe."

Gavi: The Vaccine Alliance
www.gavi.org
This international organization was set up in 2000. It aims to save lives and protect health by bringing vaccines to children around the world.

Johns Hopkins University & Medicine, Coronavirus Resource Center
https://coronavirus.jhu.edu
The Johns Hopkins University School of Medicine runs this website to keep the public, health care professionals, and policymakers informed about COVID-19. They provide the latest data on the pandemic and expert guidance to help guide preventive practices.

Kaiser Family Foundation

www.kff.org

The Kaiser Family Foundation is a nonpartisan nonprofit that conducts surveys, polls, and other research into national health issues in the United States. It has conducted in-depth research into public attitudes about COVID-19 and related policies.

National Institutes of Health

www.nih.gov

The National Institutes of Health, part of the US Department of Health and Human Services, is the agency responsible for medical research in the United States. It has provided funding to scientists and doctors seeking to understand and treat COVID-19.

World Bank

www.worldbank.org

The World Bank is an international organization that aims to reduce poverty and increase prosperity in low-income countries. The organization is involved in making access to COVID-19 vaccines more equitable around the world.

World Health Organization

www.who.int

This agency of the United Nations is responsible for coordinating worldwide efforts to respond to health emergencies, including the COVID-19 pandemic.

World Trade Organization

www.wto.org

The World Trade Organization governs trade among a group of member countries with the goal of helping to improve people's lives and raise standards of living worldwide.

For Further Research

Books

Marcia S. Gresko, *COVID-19 and the Challenges of the New Normal.* San Diego: ReferencePoint, 2021.

Debora MacKenzie, *COVID-19: The Pandemic That Never Should Have Happened and How to Stop the Next One.* New York: Hachette, 2020.

Andy Slavitt, *Preventable: The Inside Story of How Leadership Failures, Politics, and Selfishness Doomed the U.S. Coronavirus Response.* New York: St. Martin's, 2021.

Bradley Steffens, *Health, Illness, and Death in the Time of COVID-19.* San Diego: ReferencePoint, 2021.

Lynne Ternus, *Life During COVID-19.* San Diego: ReferencePoint, 2021.

Internet Sources

Bloomberg, "Prognosis: Breakthrough" (podcast), 2021. https://podcasts.apple.com.

Karleigh Frisbie Brogan, "Calling Me a Hero Only Makes You Feel Better," *The Atlantic*, April 18, 2020. www.theatlantic.com.

David Cole and Daniel Mach, "We Work at the A.C.L.U. Here's What We Think About Vaccine Mandates," *New York Times*, September 2, 2021. www.nytimes.com.

Celine Gounder, "Epidemic" (podcast), 2020–2021. www.justhumanproductions.org.

Melissa Heikkillä, "Swedish King: Country Has 'Failed' on Coronavirus Pandemic," *Politico*, December 17, 2020. www.politico.eu.

Julian C. Jamison, "Lockdowns Will Starve People in Low-Income Countries," *Washington Post*, April 20, 2020. www.washingtonpost.com.

Los Angeles Times, "How Native Americans Became a Vaccine Success Story" (podcast), September 2, 2021. www.latimes.com.

Melissa Mahtani, "I Got Vaccinated—but My Family Can't, and the Guilt Is Killing Me," CNN, April 19, 2021. www.cnn.com.

Smriti Mallapaty et al., "How COVID Vaccines Shaped 2021 in Eight Powerful Charts," *Nature News*, December 16, 2021. www.nature.com.

National Public Radio, *The Coronavirus Crisis: Everything You Need to Know about the Global Pandemic*, 2022. www.npr.org.

New York Times, "Coronavirus in the U.S.: Latest Map and Case Count," 2022. www.nytimes.com.

Emily Stewart, "Anti-maskers Explain Themselves," Vox, August 7, 2020. www.vox.com.

Index

Note: Boldface page numbers indicate illustrations.

ACLU, 22
Adams, Kathleen, 50
age and disease risk, 6
anti-vaccination (anti-vax) movement, 43–44
anxiety, 34
Aon, 31
Assefi, Nassim, 48
Association of American Medical Colleges, 41
Australia, 29

Ballotpedia, 32–33
Banks, Jim, 16–17
Barouch, Dan, 46–47
Bhandari, Esha, 18
Bhatt, Samir, 27
Biden, Joe
    on responsibility that accompanies freedom, 19
    on vaccination as best protection against
        COVID-19, 20
    vaccine mandates and, 15
BioNTech, 46
Black people
    efforts made to vaccinate, 48–49
    fear and distrust of medical system by, 42–43
    high exposure rate of, 22–23
    loss of employment, 33, **35**
    percentage vaccinated, 41
Bohnak, Karl, 17
Bonbargen, Garth, 15
breakthrough infections, 9, 44
Brogan, Karleigh Frisbie, 36
Brookings Institution, 31, 43
Business Insider (website), 28–29
Butcher, Karen, 34
Butcher, Matthew, 34

Canada, 24, 40, **42**
Cannon, Clare, 34
Carl XVI Gustaf (king of Sweden), 29
Case, Anne, 34–35
Centers for Disease Control and Prevention
    (CDC), 9, 10–11
China, lockdowns in, 28
Cole, David, 22
Commonwealth Fund, 45
Congressional Research Service, 33
COVAX program, 40, 50
COVID-19
    consequences of overcrowding in hospitals by
        unvaccinated, 20, 22

    declared pandemic, 7
    droplet spread of, 9
    ease of spread by people without symptoms,
        20
    exponential growth of, 27
    first reported to WHO, 7
    mutations of
        into more contagious variants, 8–9, 23
        vaccinations and, 44
    testing for, 37

Dearden, Nick, 44
deaths
    American (by February 2022), 8
    "deaths of despair," 34–35
    from drug overdoses, 34
    global (by February 2022), 6
    number of, prevented by vaccines, 45
    preventable, of unvaccinated people, 44
    Sweden compared to Norway, 28–29
"deaths of despair," 34–35
del Rio, Carlos, 46
Delta variant, 8–9, 44
democracy, individualism as cornerstone of, 13
depression, 34
disease risk, 6–7
domestic violence, 34

Eberl, Jason T., 23
education
    during lockdowns, 31, 33–34, 36
    spread of COVID-19 and, 34
employment
    age and race and loss of, 33, **35**
    essential workers as victims, 36
    lockdowns and, 29, 33, **35**
    remote work, 22–23, 31
    vaccine mandates and, 15, **16**, 17, 24

Fauci, Anthony, 46
"flattening the curve," 27
Food and Drug Administration (FDA), 10
Fourteenth Amendment of US Constitution, 14

Germany, **30**
Ghebreyesus, Tedros Adhanom, 39–40
Gounder, Celine, 47
Government Executive (digital publication), 17
government overreach
    mandates are, 15–18
    US Constitution limits powers of federal
        government, 15
Guo Jing, 32

Hamel, Liz, 43
handwashing, 11
Hanson, Claudia, 28–29
Harris School of Public Policy (University of
    Chicago), 35–36
Harter, Thomas D., 23
health conditions, disease risk and preexisting,
    6–7
health decisions, personal and private nature of,
    13
Hispanic people
    efforts made to vaccinate, 48–49
    high exposure rate of, 22–23
    loss of employment, 33, **35**
    vaccination of, 41
Household Pulse Survey (US Census Bureau), 34
Hsiang, Solomon, 26, 27

Imperial College London, 26–27
Indigenous communities, 49–50
individual rights
    as core American value, 13
    does not include risking harm to others, 20
    mandates violate, 12
        by employers, **16**
        right to privacy and bodily autonomy, 14–15
    public opinion about sacrifice of, to support
        common good, **21**
Inglesby, Tom, 28

Jamison, Julian C., 36
Jiles, Everett, 43–44
JobKeeper program, 29

Kaiser Family Foundation, 24, 55
Kang, Gagandeep, 47
Kluge, Hans Henri P., 45

Lancet (medical journal), 36
LaTourette, Adele H., 31
Lindsay, Sandra, **10**, 42–43
lockdowns
    have done more good than harm, 25
        examples of Germany and Sweden, **30**
        saved lives, 26–27, 28–29
        slowed spread of disease, 28
    have done more harm than good, 25
        did not stop the spread of COVID-19, 35–36
        economic harm, 33
        increase deaths from drug overdoses,
            34–35
        increase in anxiety and depression, 34
        increase in domestic violence, 34
        public opinion about, 32–33
        school closings adversely affected children
            and teenagers, 33–34
    world's first, 32
low-income communities

barriers to vaccination of residents, 41–42
    efforts made to vaccinate, 48–49
    high exposure rate of residents, 22–23, 36
low-income countries, vaccinations in, 41, **42**, 50
Lucas, Deborah, 33
Lusiani, Niko, 40–41

Mach, Daniel, 22
Mahtani, Melissa, 40
mandates
    by employers for employees to be vaccinated,
        15
    examples of, 13
    protect public health, 12
        are responsibility as citizen, 19
        consequences of overcrowding in hospitals
            by unvaccinated, 20, 22
        freedom does not include endangering
            others, 20, 22
        public opinion about sacrifice of individual
            rights to, **21**
        some vulnerable people cannot protect
            selves, 22–23
        success of, 24
        vaccination is best method to halt spread of
            COVID-19, 19–20
        voluntary vaccination programs covered fewer
            than necessary for herd immunity, 23
    by states and cities, 15–16
    violate individual rights, 12
        by employers, **16**
        right to privacy and bodily autonomy, 14–15
masks
    children and, 22
    importance of wearing, 10, 20
    mandates
        as government overreach, 13–14
        public opinion about, **21**
        states prohibiting, 16
mental health, 34
Morocho, Isai, 6
Morrison, Scott, 29
mutations, 8–9, 44

National Public Radio, 29
New York Times (newspaper), 17
Norway, 28–29

Okonjo-Iweala, Ngozi, 41
Omicron variant, 9, 44

panic, 8
Patrick, Dan, 32
Pfizer, 46
politics and vaccination, 43–44
Pollock, Bradley, 24
Powell, Colin, 22
Prabhala, Achal, 40, 44

prevention, 9–11, 10–11, 37
    See also lockdowns; masks; vaccines and
        vaccinations
public health, mandates protect, 12
    are citizens' responsibility, 19
    consequences of overcrowding in hospitals by
        unvaccinated, 20, 22
    freedom does not include endangering others,
        20, 22
    public opinion about sacrifice of individual
        rights to, **21**
    some vulnerable people cannot protect selves,
        22–23
    success of, 24
    vaccination is best method to halt spread of
        COVID-19, 19–20
    voluntary vaccination programs covered fewer
        than necessary for herd immunity, 23
public opinion
    employer vaccination mandates, **16**
    lockdowns, 32–33
    sacrifice of personal liberty to support
        common good, **21**

Ramjee, Gita, 6
Rasmussen, Scott, 32–33
Ravadge, Olivia, 15
Read, Richard, 50
Romain, Dez-Ann, 6

Sahin, Ugur, 46, 47
Sandoval, Pierre, 48–49
SARS-CoV-2 virus, 7
    See also COVID-19
Shimura, Ken, 6
Simon Fraser University (British Columbia,
    Canada), 24
South Korea, 37
spread, 9
Starling, Ganeene, 6
Stefanik, Elise, 16
Stella, Roberto, 6
Swaminathan, Soumya, 45–46
Sweden, 28–29, **30**
symptoms, 11
systemic racism, 42–43

testing, 37
Trump, Donald, 39

United Kingdom, 40, **42**
United States
    deaths (February 2022), 8
    economic aid measures during pandemic, 29
    economic recovery in, 31
    first person vaccinated, **10**
    hoarding of vaccine for own citizens by, 40–41,
        42

percentage vaccinated (January 2022), 39
    vaccine was distributed unfairly within,
        41–42
University of Chicago, 35–36
US Census Bureau, 34
US Constitution, 14, 15
US Supreme Court, 14–15

vaccines and vaccinations
    anti-vax movement, 43–44
    of Black population
        efforts made to vaccinate, 48–49
        fear and distrust of medical system by,
            42–43
        percentage of, 41
    breakthrough infections and, 9
    development of, 8, 45, 46–47
    distribution has failed, 38
        anti-vax movement claims have spread,
            43–44
        Black, Hispanic, and low-income
            communities in US had trouble getting
            vaccine, 41–42
        Black and Hispanic people have been
            vaccinated at a lower rate than Whites,
            41–43
        development of variants is proof, 44
        high- and middle-income countries
            vaccinated their citizens, 40–41, **42**
    distribution has saved lives, 38
        efforts made in low-income communities
            and communities of color, 48–49
        number of deaths prevented, 45
        number of hospitalizations prevented, 45
    fear of side effects from, 6
    first in US, **10**
    income and, 41–42
    in Indigenous communities, 49–50
    in low-income countries, 41, **42**, 50
    manufacturing of, 47
    operation of, 10
    passports indicating status, 17, 24
    rate
        global (January 2022), 46
        global (February 2022), **49**
        in US (January 2022), 39
Valdez, Josephine, 17
viruses, basic facts about, 7

Washington Post, 36
Weintraub, Rebecca, 23
Wise, Alana, 13
World Health Organization (WHO), 7
Wuhan, China, 7
Wynia, Matthew K., 23

Yale School of Public Health, 24, 35
Yentel, Diane, 29

Picture Credits

About the Author

Kathryn Hulick is the author of many books about science for teens, including *Welcome to the Future: Robot Friends, Fusion Energy, Pet Dinosaurs, and More* (about how technology could change the world in the future) and *Strange but True: 10 of the World's Greatest Mysteries Explained* (about the science and history of ghosts, aliens, and other mysterious things). In addition to writing, she enjoys hiking, gardening, painting, and reading. She weathered the pandemic safely at home in Massachusetts with her husband, son, dog, and numerous house plants.